NEW RULES

NEW RULES

Polite Musings from a Timid Observer

BILL MAHER

RODALE

Notice
Mention of specific companies, organizations, or authorities in this book does not
imply endorsement by the publisher, nor does mention of specific companies,
organizations, or authorities imply that they endorse this book.
Internet addresses and telephone numbers given in this book were accurate
at the time it went to press.

Printed in the United States of America
Rodale Inc. makes every effort to use acid-free ♾, recycled paper ♻.

Book design by Christopher Rhoads
Cover photograph by Blake Little

Library of Congress Cataloging-in-Publication Data

Maher, Bill.
    New rules : polite musings from a timid observer / Bill Maher.
        p.   cm.
    ISBN-13 978–1–59486–295–3 hardcover
    ISBN-10 1–59486–295–8 hardcover
    1. American wit and humor.   I. Title.
PN6165.M34   2005
791.45'72—dc22   2005016222

Distributed to the book trade by Holtzbrinck Publishers

2   4   6   8   10   9   7   5   3   1   hardcover

We inspire and enable people to improve their lives and the world around them
For more of our products visit **rodalestore.com** or call 800-848-4735

Acknowledgments

There are a lot of people to thank when a book comes out—the folks mentioned below are just the most prominent.

Lots of people thought a New Rules book would be a good idea, but Leigh Haber is the extraordinary editor who made it happen.

Michael Viner is the first name I think of when I think of books. He's doing the audio on this one, and any excuse to work with Mike is worth making.

Marc Gurvitz has been my manager forever and managed this book as well as he does everything. And thanks to Steve Lafferty at CAA, who got the ball rolling.

Polly Auritt of the *Real Time* staff did a great job getting the pictures we needed to help make you laugh.

And the writers of *Real Time*—Chris Kelly, Brian Jacobsmeyer, Ned Rice, Jay Jaroch, David Feldman, and Danny Vermont—are not just lol funny but know what time it is in America better than anyone I know.

Scott Carter, Sheila Griffiths, and Dean Johnsen produce *Real Time*, and their sensibility is unmistakably—thank goodness—on everything I do.

And last, but really first, is my longtime producer/head writer of *Politically Incorrect*, and now *Real Time*, the Rob Petrie to my Alan Brady, Mr. Billy Martin. New Rules was his idea. I remember the fax he sent to me in 2002 as we were gearing up to launch a new show for HBO, borne of the ashes of *Politically Incorrect*, attemping to bring along what was good about that show and leave behind what we'd outgrown. Billy suggested New Rules as a segment, and I knew right away it was a keeper. Lucky for me, he has been as well.

And, corny as it may sound, I do cherish the bond between me and the audience, the minority that follows my stuff and always makes me glad it's us against the world.

Foreword

NEW RULE

No more books by talk show hosts! No, I mean it! Just this last one and then that's it. Who do we think we are, anyway?

I guess it's not enough to broadcast our every brilliant thought to millions of viewers each week. We also have to amass compilations of our favorite, most precious *bon mots* so that people can carry them around under their arms and enjoy them at the beach or on the subway or during a quiet moment sitting alone at home in a small room. Okay, okay, and they also make great gifts. There, I've said it.

But this book is different. It's not your typical, pompous fare where I, the all-knowing host, sit in judgment, presuming to know, through my vast experience as a media whore, how you should be living your lives. No, no—not at all. This is a simple, humble collection of rules that basically points out how everyone but me has their head up their ass. Trust me, it's a great read. And have I mentioned it also makes a great gift?

But here's why I really wanted to publish this book: whenever I'm at an airport waiting for a plane to take me to some stand-up gig, a stranger will invariably approach me and say, "Excuse me, sir, could you drop your pants so we can see what the dog is sniffing at?"

And that's why I wanted to make New Rules into a book—not just so there would be something else for people to discuss with me in airports, but also because it seemed about time that this "structureless" society of ours got back to the idea of rules, limits, and boundaries.

We have come to interpret the word "freedom" as meaning "without rules or boundaries," but that's not all there is to it. Kris Kristofferson wrote, "Freedom's just another word for nothing left to lose," apparently without considering that "nothing left to lose" is not another word at all, but four words. In doing so, he followed the rules of neither math nor grammar. What a loser.

And yet, when I was a teenager, I wanted to be just like Kris Kristofferson: grizzled. And not following the rules. Rules were for squares. I thought I was too cool for rules, which is quite amusing considering nothing about me at that age even remotely suggested coolness, except maybe my plaid polyester bell-bottoms. Of course, that's often the way it is: The urge to rebel in youth often predates having a reason to do so. But then one day you take a lawn dart in the kidney and suddenly following the rules—at least the rules about lawn darts—doesn't seem like such a bad idea.

I never did take a lawn dart in the kidney—that's just an example—but I did wake up one morning after a sleepover at John Waters's house to find my sleeping bag wasn't zipped up the same way as when I passed out. We all learn. It's just a matter of how and when.

Whatever happened to all of the rules we used to live by, anyway? Before the "Me" Generation, followed by the "Me, Me, Me" Generation, followed by the "What Part of Me Don't You Understand?" Generation, there were rules—rules like "No trespassing," "No shoes, no shirt, no service," and "Please don't touch the dancers"—and they applied to everyone. Nowadays, these same rules are either ignored completely or viewed more as suggestions to be followed á la carte, depending on which ones we like.

And our respect for rules seems to be fluid, depending on convenience. Take "Do not feed the ducks." That rule would seem easy enough to follow, especially if we have no intention of feeding the ducks in the first place. But if we've come all this way with a carload of toddlers and a sack full of bread, what's a little duck feeding going to hurt? It is presumptions like that one, that rules apply more to others than to ourselves, that have placed society into disarray and Martha Stewart into an electronic ankle bracelet.

Even our trusted leaders can't be counted on to observe the rules—or at least they do so only selectively. "Rule of law!" Remember that popular refrain from the days of the Clinton impeachment? As House Republicans told us at the time, they really had no choice. It was all out of their hands. Legislators are bound to uphold the rules as they're written, no matter what—except, apparently, as they apply to subpoenaing the brain dead. And by "the brain dead," of course, I mean baseball's Mark McGwire.

Rules are the signposts that define where our rights end and those of our fellow citizens begin. Adhering to rules and abiding by a code of civility—this is what separates us from the apes . . . and Tom DeLay. Stop following the rules and you start stepping on toes. And that's where this book comes in—not necessarily to rehash our old, out-of-date rules but to establish new ones for a self-obsessed, success-by-any-means, get-mine culture. These are the rules that, frankly, were not necessary back when we practiced those old-fashioned time wasters: courtesy, consideration, and common sense.

Rules are important—we all need them. They provide structure and help us to know where we stand with others. That's why I'm constantly fighting with my neighbors—no rules. Okay, and because the makeup sex is fantastic. When we disregard the rules altogether we get anarchy or, worse yet, Enron.

Of course, children need structure and rules, too. I've always said the three most important things for a child to learn are respect, accountability, and to shut the hell up on airplanes. Rules help shape kids and let them know that they're loved. Children not subject to these healthy boundaries often find themselves, by the time they are teenagers, lacking any real sense of security or self. These kids are destined, sadly, for social difficulties, school shootings, or, even more likely, session after session of red-hot car sex with their French teacher.

Children, though, who are exposed to the healthy, enforced rules of conscientious parenting seem to grow to their "right size," complete with a moral compass. There is no limit to how far a child can go with just a little discipline and structure. Just look at what the Hitler Youth did for the pope.

So, then, here you have them—my New Rules for a better world, for all of you out there who love freedom but still crave a little structure. This book, come to think of it, is a lot like having to drop your pants at the airport: There's an important point to it, but mostly it's just plain funny. So, enjoy it! And did I mention, it also makes a great gift?

BILL MAHER

NEW RULES

A Perfect Cliché

NEW RULE

Stop calling it a "perfect storm" when two bad things happen at the same time. Sometimes it's just some crap happening at the same time as some other crap. Let's go back to what we used to call it before that movie about George Clooney and his epic struggle to kill more tuna: Shit happens.

AND NEW RULE

I don't care that your phone takes pictures. It's a phone, not a Swiss Army knife. Great, now the annoying camera buff and the annoying cell phone prick can merge as one guy. Hey, if you can figure out how to make that "camera phone" play country-western music real loud, we could call it "a perfect storm of assholes."

A Suit and Battery

NEW RULE

Now that you've won and you're safe, you have to tell us: What the hell was that thing on your back during the debate?

AARP Yours

NEW RULE

Stop fucking with old people. Target is introducing a redesigned pill bottle—it's square, with a bigger label, and the top is now the bottom. And by the time Grandpa figures out how to open it, his ass will be in the morgue. Congratulations, Target, you've just solved the Social Security crisis.

Abigail Van Buried

NEW RULE

Dead people can't write advice columns. Dear Abby has been dead for years, yet she continues her daily syndicated column. If I want to hear what a corpse thinks, I'll read Robert Novak.

Abu Grab-Ass

NEW RULE

Lynndie England and Charles Graner should not be sentenced to jail. They should be photographed performing sex acts, stacked in a pile of naked people, and stripped of their dignity. Or as it's better known here, *The Real World*.

Accessories after the Fact

NEW RULE

Martha Stewart does not need an electronic ankle bracelet. There's a caravan of news vans on her driveway, choppers overhead, and paparazzi with telephoto lenses in the trees—where the hell is she gonna go? Plus, what sense does it make to remand a "home diva" to her home? That's like sentencing Kirstie Alley to check in nightly at IHOP.

Ad-Nauseum

NEW RULE

Stop running TV ads I don't understand. I'm not sure if IBM's latest is advertising weapons of mass destruction or stool softener. Then there's the one with clouds moving in fast motion, some Buddhist monks on a cell phone, and James Earl Jones saying, "We're the world leader in virtual network upstream data retrieval." What?! Hey, fuck you. I watch TV to see bimbos marry strangers for money. If I want to be confused, I'll take mushrooms.

But Siriusly

NEW RULE

Paying to listen to the radio is wrong. Seemingly normal Americans are now paying 10 dollars a month to get satellite radio. That's right—they're paying to listen to the radio. Hello! It's the radio! The whole point of radio is that you don't have to pay for it. It's like paying to hum. If it wasn't free, do you think they'd play Foghat? So what if satellite radio has a hundred channels. So does cable TV, and just like cable TV, 5 of them are good, 20 suck, and the rest are in Spanish.

Butt Out

NEW RULE

Sodomy rules! If it's still asking too much to legalize the blow job, let's start with medicinal blow jobs and work from there. What two consenting adults choose to do in the privacy of a casting office is their business.

Byte Me

N E W   R U L E

Computers aren't for voting; they're for picking up underage girls. Voting by computer sounds really cool and futuristic—if this were 1969. But now that we all have computers, we know that they are, in fact, huge fuck-up machines. They're like having a compact, silicon version of Gary Busey on your desk—you never know what's going to happen. I'll tell you what'll happen: Some 13-year-old hacker in Finland is going to hand the presidency to Kylie Minogue. You thought the 2004 election was bad—wait until the next one is decided by a customer service rep in New Delhi.

Truth in Labeling

Stop believing slogans, especially the ones that come out of the White House. Twinkies aren't wholesome goodness, and the "Clear Skies Initiative" isn't really going to bring clear skies. And it turns out that the "No Child Left Behind" law actually leaves lots of children behind. It leaves so many behind, in fact, that they have a name for them now: "pushouts," as in "we're pushing you out of school so that our cumulative test scores will be higher."

Yes, that's what this is all about. Our "No Child Left Behind" law is written like this: As a state, you get federal money for your schools, but only when two main things happen—you make test scores go up and dropout rates go down. How best to achieve both of those goals? By making the dumber kids . . . disappear!

The "Texas Miracle" in education, it turns out, was all about raising test scores by making almost the entire bottom half of the class drop out, and then falsely lowering the dropout rate by putting those students in phony categories like "transferred" or "enrolled in GED" or "dating Demi Moore."

We weren't actually improving the system, but we were making it look like we were where it matters: on paper. It's not for nothing that all those Texans looked up to Enron. For the 2000 election, Houston's dropout rate was given as 1.5 percent. After the election, it was revised to *40 percent*, probably by the same guy who makes up the budget. I don't need a degree in fuzzy math to know that 40 percent is not "no child left behind."

And if you say "no child" in your law, it takes a Texas-size nerve to then treat those kids like cards in a gin rummy game, where you get to ditch the two low ones, and where bodies just disappear like dissidents in Argentina or that Heather Locklear airport drama.

George Bush ran for office as the education guy, and his caring about leaving no child behind is what softened him into a compassionate conservative. So it seems wrong to find out that what we're really doing is just handing lots of kids a GED kit and telling them, "Good luck exploring your other educational opportunities, like learning how many vials of crack you can carry in your underwear."

As no one could tell you better than our president himself, we don't all blossom early in life, so maybe writing off so many kids so early isn't so wise. It might amuse the President to know that this is exactly what they do in his favorite country, France, but France has more of a social safety net than we do. Our safety net has a name. It's called prison.

People say education is the cornerstone of our democracy—they're wrong, of course. The cornerstone of our democracy is campaign cash and lots of it. But shouldn't education still count for something? As the president himself might say, "We can do gooder."

BILL MAHER

NEW RULES

C3 Pee-Yew

NEW RULE

You can stop releasing *Star Wars* now. We've seen it. I don't care if it's in a box set, if it's remastered or redigitized, if there are bonus scenes or a director's commentary; it's still a space movie for guys who can't get laid.

Call Hating

NEW RULE

Ass-kissing must be done in person. Yes, I'll "continue to hold" but not because you said, "Your call is important to us." If my call was really important to you, you'd hire a human to pick up the damn phone.

Can You Hear Me Now?

NEW RULE

No more cell phones in movie theaters. You're not a cardiologist on call—you're a putz whose babysitter wants to know where the ketchup is. And then you tell her, in the middle of the movie! Sometimes it's so loud in the theater, I can barely hear what the black people are yelling at the screen. There's a simple solution: Put your cell phone on vibrate and then up your ass.

Car Tune Network

NEW RULE

Keep your homemade mix CDs to yourself. I know you spent weeks trying to pick the perfect song to put between "Hey Ya" and "Who Let the Dogs Out," but I don't even like music. I only wear an iPod to avoid talking to you.

Cell Lout

NEW RULE

Don't call me when you're stuck in traffic. It's not my fault radio sucks. And did it ever occur to you that there wouldn't be so much traffic if people like you put down the phone and concentrated on the road? Besides, I can't talk now—I'm in the car behind you, trying to watch a DVD.

Center Old

NEW RULE

Just because you used to be famous doesn't mean you belong in *Playboy*. A recent issue features a photo spread with Debbie Gibson, perfectly nice woman, whose "electric youth" ended in 1988. Here's a way to tell if you're an '80s icon who shouldn't be naked: When you sit down, your "leg warmers" are your tits. If I want to be exposed to has-been pop stars, I'll sleep over at Neverland.

Check Your Local Lispings

N E W   R U L E

Enough with "gay-sploitation" TV. *Queer Eye for the Straight Guy?* If I want a bunch of gay men in queeny outfits telling me how to live my life, I'll go back to MASS.

Checkout Whine

N E W   R U L E

I'm not the cashier! By the time I look up from sliding my card, entering my PIN number, pressing "Enter," verifying the amount, deciding, "No, I don't want cash back," and pressing "Enter" again, the kid who's supposed to be ringing me up is standing there eating my Almond Joy. Paper? Plastic? I don't have time for that! I've just been called to do cleanup on aisle nine.

Chief Wannabe

NEW RULE

If you have to tell me what fraction of you is Native American, you're not really an Indian. There's a word for people who claim to be one-quarter Indian: Puerto Rican.

Chock Full o' Putz

NEW RULE

The more complicated the Starbucks order, the bigger the asshole. If you walk into a Starbucks and order a decaf grande half-soy half-low-fat iced-vanilla double-shot gingerbread cappuccino extra dry light ice with one Sweet'N Low and one NutraSweet . . . you're a huge asshole. If you're this much of a control freak about coffee, you must be really unbearable when it comes to something important, like a Danish.

Chopping Spree

NEW RULE

If you don't want the world to think your religion is medieval, stop beheading people. Texans are bloodthirsty and dim, and even they learned to
use an electric chair. Come on, Islam. Join the nineteenth century.

LAX Security

NEW RULE

Homeland Security can't call itself Homeland Security until it provides
homeland security.

According to an FBI report, airlines are still a prime target for al-Qaeda,
mainly because airline security in America remains a faith-based initiative.
President Bush has certainly proved himself resolute when he wants to
make something an issue—so we really could use his steely resolve on this
one. Or, to paraphrase Judge Judy, "Don't pee on my leg and tell me you're
a bomb-sniffing dog."

As a comedian, I do a lot of flying, and some of it is in airplanes, which
unfortunately only leave from airports, which have become bureaucratic
nightmares that test our patience, our sense of logic, and our ability to hide
a small brick of hash inside a hollowed-out can of deodorant.

If you're looking for a reason terrorists haven't hijacked another plane, I
think I know what it is: It's too much of a hassle! I mean seriously, people,
I'm on the road a lot—sometimes I honestly can't remember who packed
my bag!

Did you hear the latest? Now there can be no lighters on planes. This, of
course, will do nothing to change the safety equation, but it will ensure that

Class-Holes

Stop giving me that pop-up ad for Classmates.com. There's a reason you don't talk to people for 25 years—because you don't particularly like them. Besides, I already know what the captain of the football team is doing these days—mowing my lawn.

if the passengers end up enjoying the terrorists' work, they still can't bring them back for an encore.

And the new luggage screening system, which everyone agrees would help a lot, remains on the drawing board because the Bush administration insists the airlines should pay for it. Are they high? The airlines are broker than Michael Jackson. Delta announced last week it was taking away the pillows—*the pillows?* That's like Holiday Inn saying they can't afford the mint. Plus, now what am I supposed to use to muffle the crying kid next to me?

There's what we pay lip service to, and then there's what we pay money for, which is, after all, what we actually "value." We could have good security at the airport; we know how to do it. Have you ever been to a casino? There are more cameras than at a Korean wedding, with zoom lenses that can count the stitches on your date's sex change from 50 feet away. You can't do math in your head in a casino without being spotted, recorded on videotape, hustled off the floor, and buried in the desert by Joe Pesci.

So what I'm saying is, Am I just a dreamer, or could we try to make the airports at least as secure as Circus Circus?

Closed-Mouth Session

NEW RULE

Congressional sing-alongs of "God Bless America" are the cheapest form of political pandering. We get it. You're on our side. Now get back to work. Those lobbyists in your office aren't going to blow themselves.

Don't Play It Again, Sam

NEW RULE

Everyone has to stop pretending Woody Allen movies don't completely suck. Hollywood stars must stop pretending that it's an honor to appear in his unwatchable, recycled tripe, and critics have to stop pretending that a tiny old Jew could be scoring with Tea Leoni and Helen Hunt. Somebody contact wardrobe—the emperor has no clothes.

Du Jour Job

NEW RULE

Room service personnel must know what the soup is! You're working the phones at room service. What do you think you're going to get asked—what you're wearing? If I'm paying 28 dollars for two eggs and a Coke, you should know the soup, all the state capitals, and where I left my keys.

Not Another Teen Movie

NEW RULE

Somebody make a movie I want to go see. If you're asking why movies have gotten so bad, I'll tell you why: It's because Hollywood studios now get 60 percent of their money from DVDs, all of which are bought by the young, dumb male demographic, the same one that's given us *Maxim* magazine, attention deficit disorder, and George Bush.

When I was a teenager, Hollywood didn't give a damn about me—and that was good! Good for the movies and good for me because I was challenged—to smarten up instead of dumbing down. Besides ruining movies, we've also managed to ruin our kids by making everything be about them. And now if I want to see a movie, I had better like loud noises, things blowing up, and Colin Farrell.

Movies suck because Hollywood has figured out that Mom and Dad don't spend their money on movies anymore; they give their money to their kids and *they* spend it on movies—to break up their shopping sprees at the mall. It's like American parents are on one long date with their kids—no, it's even worse; it's like Robert DeNiro in *Casino*, helplessly trying to buy the love of a shopaholic hooker with no heart, played, of course, by Sharon Stone.

Before I die, could someone please make one more movie I want to go see? I'm not asking for the moon here, and I'm not some film snob with a ponytail who only likes subtitled Albanian documentaries. But to middle-aged people like me, a good movie is like good sex—you don't have to put one out every day, but when whole seasons go by without getting one, you do start to get a little horny for entertainment.

BILL MAHER

NEW RULES

Eddie Iz

NEW RULE

Transvestites are gay. I know what you're going to say: "Bill, not all transvestites are gay." Yes, they are. Studies show . . . aw, screw studies. Yes, they are.

Elimistate

NEW RULE

The next reality show must be called *America's Stupidest State*. We'll start at 50, and each week, if your state does something really stupid with, say, evolution or images of the Virgin Mary, you'll move on to the next round. Of course, the final five will always end up being Alabama, Utah, Kansas, Texas, and Florida. Sorry, Tennessee.

Emerald Ale

NEW RULE

This St. Patrick's Day—if you want to get drunk, just get drunk. Don't blame Ireland. Why is the drunk the only Irish icon we celebrate on March 17? What about the unreadable novelist, the unwatchable playwright, the unbearable clog dancer? Or the fat cop, the crooked mayor, the shifty bomber, the incompetent waitress, the fiery spinster schoolmarm, the dowdy upstairs maid, and the sadistic lesbian nun?

Emission Impossible

NEW RULE

Dating a self-proclaimed 26-year-old virgin is probably not the best way to stifle the gay rumors. You're a big star, you can have any woman you want, and you pick the one actress in town who doesn't put out? I thought Scientology was supposed to *clear* your mind.

Entertainment Weakly

NEW RULE

No more TV gambling. First, there was *Celebrity Poker*, then there was *Celebrity Blackjack*. I saw one show that was just Camryn Manheim scratching lottery tickets. What gets on TV has to be at least as interesting as what's on the average security monitor at a convenience store.

Exit Pole

NEW RULE

Don't lop off your boyfriend's penis and flush it down the toilet. That's what Kim Tran of Anchorage, Alaska, did recently after she and her boyfriend had a spat: She cut off his penis and flushed it down the toilet. Whatever happened to the silent treatment?

Exit, Poll

NEW RULE

Stop taking stupid polls. Every little news program on every cable news network has their own dumb-ass online poll. And it's always some ridiculous question like, "We want to know what you think. Is John Bolton too much of an asshole, not enough of an asshole, or just the right amount of asshole?" This is America. Knowing nothing and choosing one of two options isn't a poll. It's an election.

Assisted Leaving

NEW RULE

Just because you have a job for life doesn't mean you have to do it for life. It's well and proper that we venerate our elders—but give it a freakin' rest. To every thing, there is a season. Turn! Turn! Turn! A time to reap, a time to sow. And a time to pack it in, put on a housecoat, and fall asleep in front of the Golf Channel.

Now, I know it must be hard to give up your job when your job is literally sitting on a throne, or being on a "supreme" court, or keeping women out of your priesthood to make room for the gays—but at some point it starts to look like you think of yourself as indispensable, and no one is indispensable, including you, the late Mr. Infallible. I don't want to say the pope was out of it, but at the end he was caught saying two Our Fathers and three *Proud Marys*.

And Queen Elizabeth, your son has been waiting so long to be king, even his mistress is a senior citizen. Queen for 50-plus years, it's a good run—second only to *Cats*. But now it's time to kick off those royal slippers, smell the English roses, and spend some time with those Nazi grandkids.

I don't understand America. We work until we have strokes, then after we die, our estates are fought over, and we're turned into Soylent Green and eaten.

You know who knows how to live? Titans of industry: Ray Kroc, Colonel Sanders, Dave from Wendy's—none of them spent their golden years tied to a desk. They all died of heart disease from eating their own food.

In conclusion, there's a reason that names like Cary Grant, Joe DiMaggio, and Johnny Carson inspire a special kind of awe: They all did something that made them more beloved than anyone else—they left before we got sick of them. They didn't make us all pretend to yawn to get them to leave the party. They looked around, as all of us will someday, and said, I've done my part, I've said my piece, and I'm finally deaf enough to stand being home all day with my spouse.

BILL MAHER

NEW RULES

Face Reality

NEW RULE

Stop being shocked when reality TV contestants turn out to be wife beaters, drug addicts, shoplifters, and porn stars. They're letting us marry them to strangers and make them eat eel shit. They don't have the gene for shame—that's why they're on reality shows.

Faking the Band

NEW RULE

No playing guitar and harmonica at the same time. Yes, I know it's possible, but it always sounds like shit, and you look like an idiot doing it. If you must have both playing at the same time, hire another musician. How much can a harmonica player cost? Wearing a harmonica harness is only acceptable if you make a living performing in the subway, and you have cymbals strapped to your knees.

Fantastic Bore

NEW RULE

Let's make at least every second American movie not based on a comic book. How many of you knew the film *Sideways* was actually based on a comic book called *The Tedious Adventures of Drunk Man and Horny*? If we keep making superhero movies, the rest of the world is going to start seeing America as some kind of infantile fantasyland where reality is whatever we say it is and all our problems can be solved with violence.

Faux Paw

NEW RULE

Don't make people who hate you hug you. Whatever the Bush administration is blackmailing John McCain with, stop.

Fashion Police

N E W   R U L E

Give arrested celebrities a chance to comb before their mug shots are taken! Not allowing fallen icons to wash up gives the impression that they're, well, washed up.

And we'd hate for that to happen.

Felonious Monks

NEW RULE

If you're bringing birthday cake to a chimp, bring enough for everyone. An L.A. man visiting a chimpanzee in a wildlife sanctuary was mauled by the other chimps when he didn't bring any cake for them. The man's face was partially peeled off and his nose was completely detached. And, in this town, that kind of work costs good money.

Femoirs

NEW RULE

You don't get a million dollars just for being gay. Remember Dick Cheney's daughter Mary? The one John Kerry mentioned was a lesbian and the Republicans pretended to get irate? Well, she got a million dollar advance to write her "memoirs." Memoirs? Chapter One: "My Dad's Vice President." Chapter Two: "I Like Pussy." The End.

Film Boff

NEW RULE

Let the drive-in movie die. The popcorn is always stale, the sound is always crappy, and the picture is always blurry. It's 2005—teens no longer have to drive onto a hillside and park in formation to get a hand job.

Flat Tax

I don't care how big or flat it is, it's still just a TV. Congratulations—you just paid $10,000 to watch *Hogan's Heroes*.

Floral Sex

NEW RULE

"Valentine's Day Sex" is an urban legend. Every Valentine's Day ad is the same pitch: Buy her the roses and candy, and you'll get the "Valentine's Day Sex." Unfortunately, lust, over time, is just like the roses and the candy—wilting and growing stale. The last time a guy actually got sex for chocolate was when we liberated France.

Folk Off

NEW RULE

Bob Dylan must stop denying he was the voice of a generation. Bob, that's not something you get to decide. It's fate and you were it. If your generation could actually choose a voice, don't you think they'd have picked one better than yours?

Fool Recovery

NEW RULE

Former drug addicts and alcoholics have to stop saying, "I almost died." No. Cancer survivors almost died. You almost had too good a time.

For Your Reconsideration

NEW RULE

Take one back. Every year, along with handing out the Oscars, the Academy should take one back. Get someone up there to say, "We blew it. Roberto Benigni—give it back! We just got you out of your seat that year because we wanted to see you dry-hump Judi Dench."

Ford Galaxy

NEW RULE

No SUVs in space. The new space plane isn't a triumph of the spirit, it's a low-orbit midlife crisis. Space tourism is God's way of telling you you're not spending enough on lap dances, baccarat, and cocaine.

Forget Paris

NEW RULE

Talentless teenagers who exist to amuse us must keep up in the battle to be the dippiest twit. First Paris Hilton's topless cell phone pictures ended up on the Internet; isn't it about time Britney Spears did something trashy? Come on, honey, use your imagination. I don't know—let the wind blow your pants off, or have a miscarriage in a liquor store, or get a de-vorce from Butthead. The ball's in your trailer court.

Fossett Drip

NEW RULE

The next time Steve Fossett tries to fly something around the world, shoot him down. First it was a balloon. Then it was a plane. Next he'll try to do it strapped to a giant kite. Steve, we get it. You don't like spending time with your wife. But getting caught in the jet stream is not an accomplishment. It's just what clouds do. You want to spend your millions on a worthless cause, try donating it to the Democrats.

Fox Populi

NEW RULE

It's not a town hall meeting if you only invite people who promise to kiss your ass. Recently, three people at a Bush "social security town hall" were thrown out because organizers didn't like the bumper sticker on their car. This isn't good for America, and it's not even good for Bush. If all he wants to do is talk to someone who agrees with him on everything, he should go back and re-debate Kerry.

French Whine

NEW RULE

No more bitching about the French. At least they're standing up to the Bush administration, which is more than I can say for the Democrats. And it doesn't make me un-American to say I'd rather live in Paris than in some place where cheese only comes in individually wrapped slices.

Fresh Seamen

NEW RULE

England doesn't have to go out of its way to get gays in its navy. The British Navy is planning a special recruiting drive, including ads in gay men's magazines. *A-hoooy*. You're the British Navy. If you were any gayer, you'd be the White House press corps.

Friends to the End

NEW RULE

The end of *Friends* is not a national tragedy. It is just a sitcom that went off the air. One week Darren was complaining to Samantha about Larry Tate, the next week he wasn't. And nobody cared. Each character on *Friends* has fucked every other character in every possible combination, including that monkey. Let it go already.

California Hatin'

NEW RULE

Lay off California. The rest of America loves to laugh at crazy California, but let's remember this: California has a lot of people. And the reason it does is that lots of people from other states end up saying, "Fuck this, I'm outta here," and then they come here, where people ask them, "Don't you miss the winters?" No, strangely enough, I don't, just like I don't miss a car door slamming on my hand.

Make fun of California, but if it weren't for California, East Coast rappers would have to shoot musicians from Branson. If it weren't for California, there'd be almost no TV, and you'd have to go home at night and actually talk to your family.

The rest of America feels about California the way the rest of the world feels about America. They hate us because we do what we want to do. Just the way people think Americans are too blessed and too free, and it makes them nuts in the dreary hovels of Kabul and Tikrit and Lubbock, Texas. They pray to their threadbare gods that we'll get what we deserve, but it won't happen because we'll always keep you guessing.

We elected Ronald Reagan and Jerry Brown. We're home to Disney and also to *Hustler*. *The Partridge Family* and the Manson Family. We can drink a Mudslide and a Sex on the Beach during an actual mudslide while having sex on the beach. Our farms feed the world and Calista Flockhart lives here.

We have bears and great white sharks and even our washed-up actors are allowed to kill one blonde chick. We invented surfing and cyberporn and LSD and the boob job. And if we didn't, we would have.

We have oranges. Free oranges. Everywhere. What grows on the trees in Scranton?

We have a real hockey team named after a hockey team in a movie. We give our illegal aliens driver's licenses. We have a governor who digs group sex.

Would anywhere else in America trade places with L.A. or San Francisco in a piss-soaked New York minute? You bet they would, because I don't re-call anyone writing a song called "I Wish They All Could Be Rhode Island Girls."

Gas Bags

NEW RULE

The big oil companies must stop running ads telling us how much they're doing for the environment. We get it: You rape the earth, but you cuddle afterward. It's insulting—like a serial killer dumping a body by the roadside and then adopting a highway. If you folks at Shell really are serious about cleaning something up, start with your restrooms.

Gay-per-View

NEW RULE

The Bravo network has to come out of the closet. First it was *Boy Meets Boy*, then *Queer Eye for the Straight Guy*, and now their newest offering: *Manhunt*, where male models skydive in their underwear. Hey, one sign your network may be gay is when it's literally raining men. One guy actually tried to score with another in midair—but his chute wouldn't open.

Gaydar Aid

NEW RULE

No more studies trying to prove that homosexuality is genetic. This week Swedish sex researchers—and honestly, are there any other kind?—found that when exposed to male pheromones, a gay man's brain reacts differently than a straight man's. Hmm. And all this time I thought my aversion to fisting and rim-jobs came from a persuasive essay in *The New Republic*. Of course it's genetic. The only people left who don't think you're born gay are Pat Robertson and Anne Heche. Can we just leave the raving lunatics behind so we can catch up to the Europeans already?

Getting Blown

NEW RULE

Don't live close to the sea. If you build your home in a place where weather knocks houses over, weather will knock your house over. People who live in the Land of Oz have houses drop on them all the time. You don't see them marching into Emerald City demanding a handout, do you? I'm sorry a big wind came and blew everything away but the La-Z-Boy and the orange velvet pool table, but hurricanes are God's way of saying, "Get off my property!"

Gin Dummy

NEW RULE

Anyone elected mayor of a place called Sin City is allowed to be a drunk. Las Vegas mayor Oscar Goodman is taking flak for telling schoolchildren that he doesn't have a drinking problem because, quote, "I love to drink," then adding that if he had to pick anything to be stranded with on a desert island, he would bring his favorite scotch. Kids, personally I would bring Eve. Because you know that freak is packing weed.

Giving Good Headlines

NEW RULE

Using the phrase "He's ba-a-a-a-ck" is over. He's ba-ack, she's ba-ack, it's ba-ack—all over. Attention people who write mini headlines for cable news: Next time you have to write one referring to Deep Throat, the swallows of Capistrano, or some rock star's hepatitis C, spend an extra 30 seconds coming up with something original like, "Hey, does it take a spike through the heart to kill off Al Gore, this grotesque freak of nature?"

Glutton, Honey

NEW RULE

Sumo wrestling isn't a sport, it's an eating disorder. You can't call yourself an athlete if your idea of getting into shape is tripling in size. Except in baseball.

Gone Fission

NEW RULE

Sometimes "sorry" just doesn't cut it. Pakistan says it's really, really sorry for selling nuclear secrets to anyone with cash and/or a thing for Allah. That's nice. When one of their customers turns Washington into a debris field, it'll be comforting to know Islamabad feels Islama-terrible. I know putting loose nukes in play isn't a serious Muslim offense, like letting women wear pants, but here in the land of the Great Satan, it's the second most horrifying thing we can imagine.

Got MILF?

NEW RULE

You can't call your show *Wife Swap* unless the other guy really gets to bang your wife. I didn't sign up for an hour of watching Mom do some other family's laundry.

Grandma Poses

NEW RULE

Posing nude is for people who look good naked, period—not for people who look good naked *for their age*. There's a *Playboy* edition you don't wanna miss: "Girls of the AARP." One sign you may not be pinup material—if you yourself have centerfolds.

Gun Fighters

NEW RULE

Know your enemies. The National Rifle Association posted a list of antigun organizations on its Web site so NRA members would know who's against the NRA. The list includes: the Ambulatory *Pediatric* Association, the American *Medical* Association, the American Association of *Surgery*, the American *Trauma* Society, the American Academy of *Child Psychiatry*, the *Children's* Defense Fund, the Congress of Neurological Surgeons, the National Association of *School Psychologists*.

Hmm. What could all these organizations have in common? Oh yeah! *They're sick of cleaning up after the NRA!*

Gyro Worship

NEW RULE

Rejected *American Idol* contestant Constantine Maroulis must be destroyed. He kept coming on to me through my television set. I don't know why you singled me out, Constantine Maroulis, but I didn't fall for it. Sure, you may have the smoky, sexy voice of a rock-and-roll bad boy, the lean stature of a Greek god, and a sultry gaze that makes my loins stir, *but that doesn't make me gay*. Call me.

Panned Parenthood

NEW RULE

Parents have to stop coddling their children. I've heard that now some schools have stopped grading papers with red ink because of complaints that a big, mean red X is too negative—why, a kid might even think he got that question wrong. Parents today are so fixated on protection, it's amazing they ever got pregnant in the first place.

A recent reality show called *Supernanny* placed an old-school, discipline-wielding nanny into a family where the mother can't figure out that the reason she's having a nervous breakdown is that she says things to her kids like, "Tyler, Mommy would really appreciate it if you didn't throw rocks at me."

Moms and dads these days are like the Democratic Party: lame, spineless, and not holding up their end of the equation. And kids are like the Republicans: drunk with power and out of control.

Maybe that's why there's also a new phenomenon called parent coaching, a kind of tech-support service for clueless parents when their 3-year-old goes haywire. As described in a recent *New York Times* article, here are some of the questions a typical mom asks her parenting coach: What should she do when Skylar won't do his chores? Should there be limits on how he spends his allowance? Should Forrest get dessert if he does not eat a healthy dinner?

Now, for those of you who are saying, "But Bill, you're not a parent," I say true, but I have one thing these parents apparently don't: a brain. This is not rocket science. What should you do when Skylar won't do his chores? How about using your size advantage? Make him!

Because if there's one thing we know about kids, it's that if you give them an inch, the authorities will raid your Neverland Ranch. Like Michael Jackson, parents these days act like they're on a date with their children—trying to impress them, trying to buy their love, and never contradicting them or giving them a big red X when they're wrong.

So no, I don't have kids, and you know what? I don't intend to have any until people start making some I'd want my kids to play with. Until then, I'm just glad I own a lot of stock in Ritalin.

BILL MAHER

NEW RULES

Hair Apparent

NEW RULE

Dye your moustache to match your toupee. You're the new U.S. ambassador to the UN, not manager of the month at Baskin-Robbins.

Hajj-Podge

NEW RULE

Update the Hajj. Every year, the words "Islamic" and "stampede" seem to appear in the same sentence when millions of Muslims descend upon Mecca to observe what's called the Hajj. I don't understand Arabs: You've got most of the oil in the world, and your religion involves walking? Next year, I want to see a looser Hajj with a cooler name, like Allahpalooza.

Hallowed Grounds

NEW RULE

Stop telling me not to talk to you until you've had your coffee, you pathetic junkie. In fact, I'll make a deal with you: I won't talk to you *before* you've had your coffee if you won't talk to me *after* you've had your coffee.

Handicrapped

NEW RULE

If you're blind, you don't have to pick up your guide dog's poop. In California, a blind couple went to court over complaints that they didn't. You see, they would have, but they can't see shit!

Have It Yahweh

NEW RULE

God is a waffler. Pat Robertson said God told him that Iraq would be a bloody disaster. But the same God told George Bush it wouldn't, which so surprised Robertson, he almost dropped the pennies he was stealing off a dead woman's eyes. But why is God talking out of two sides of his mouth? Flip-flop. God told us to beat our swords into plowshares. God: Wrong on defense, wrong for America.

Heir Head

NEW RULE

You can't be famous for nothing. Paris Hilton can't be in the papers anymore unless she kills someone, marries J.Lo, or OD's. Also, her head is too small and she only has one facial expression.

I know that's not a rule, but someone has to say it.

AND NEW RULE

If most of the pictures on your camera phone are of yourself, you need to develop some outside interests. Someone hacked into Paris Hilton's cell phone and discovered that all of her pictures are of herself. It's almost like she's an idiot. That kind of self-love isn't healthy. Lindsey Lohan loves booze, but even she occasionally buys a round for the house.

Hin-Don't

NEW RULE

McDonald's and yoga don't mix. McDonald's has a new ad that features a sinewy woman in yoga poses. And you can tell she's just eaten McDonald's because after she gets in the lotus position, she farts. Stop trying to convince me you're not the place that almost killed Morgan Spurlock. If I want to eat healthy, I'll go to a place that serves actual food.

Suture Self

NEW RULE

Stop saying that blue state people are "out of touch" with the values and morals of the red states. I'm not out of touch with them; I just don't share them. In fact—and I know this is about 140 years late—but to the southern states I would say, upon further consideration, you can go. I know that's what you always wanted, and we've reconsidered, so go ahead. And take Texas with you. You know what they say: If at first you don't secede, try, try again. Give my regards to President Charlie Daniels.

Sorry, I almost forgot—we're in a time of healing. The time when blue states and red states come together because we have so much to offer each other. Spice Rack? Meet Gun Rack. Picky about Bottled Water? Say hello to Drinks from a Garden Hose. Bought an Antique Nightstand at an Estate Sale? Meet Uses a Giant Wooden Spool He Stole from the Phone Company as a Coffee Table.

Sorry, there I go again—kidding, when I should be healing. But sometimes I just don't understand this country. I don't get that your air is poison and your job is gone and your son is scattered all over a desert you can't find on a map, but what really matters is boys kissing.

Say what you will about the Republicans, they do stand for something. Okay, it's Armageddon, but it's something. Democrats, on the other hand, have been coasting for years on Tom Daschle's charisma, but that's just not enough anymore.

Historical Blindness

NEW RULE

Not everything is a conspiracy. Black History Month is in February because Abraham Lincoln and Frederick Douglass were born in February, not because it's the shortest month. Here's the deal: You accept this on faith, and we'll pretend you didn't completely make up Kwanzaa.

Democrats will never win another election in America if they keep trying to siphon off votes from the Republicans. They'll only win by creating a lot more Democrats, and you don't do that by trying to leach on to issues that you should be denouncing. You wind up in a goose-hunting outfit a week before the election, trying to appeal to guys who would sooner vote for the goose.

These folks aren't undecideds; they're not in play. No, what the Democrats need are fresh, new ideas that are stupid, base, and hateful enough to win voters over. I dunno, like: no drinking on Christmas. Or a constitutional amendment protecting the song "God Bless America." The death penalty for missing Mother's Day. Let's put a fetus on the dollar bill—with Reagan! You know what country has been asking for an ass kicking in the worst way? Wales.

Yes, Democrats need a really, really, really stupid, meaningless, and utterly symbolic issue. And by "issue," of course, I mean "thing to hate." How about this: an amendment that says people with fish don't have the right to call themselves pet owners. Pet owning will be legally interpreted only as owning a cat or a dog. My opponent may disagree, but that's because he's a fag.

So, Democrats and Liberals, stop saying you're going to move out of the country because Bush won. Real Liberals should be *pledging to stay* because Bush won. Trust me, you can't get away from Bush by moving to France— that's where we're invading next.

Holy Matrimony

NEW RULE

Priests should be allowed to marry. What better way to ensure celibacy?

Holy Spirit

NEW RULE

The government doesn't have time to worry about cheerleaders. The Texas senate just passed a law against "overtly sexual" cheerleading. This is a horrible law. For one thing, how do these people think we train our next generation of strippers? I'm sorry, but the only time anyone in government should be spending time on cheerleaders is when his wife is away and he's actually on a cheerleader.

Home Chopping Network

NEW RULE

Beheading hostages has jumped the shark. Come on, guys, you've seen one blurry home video of a guy in an orange jumpsuit begging for his life, you've seen them all. You've got to come up with a new twist, like one of the hostages is gay but the others don't know it, or the hostages compete for immunity . . . something. By the same token, Donald Trump has to start firing people by sawing off their heads.

Homicidal Namiacs

NEW RULE

No more serial killers with initials for nicknames, like the "bind, torture, kill" killer, BTK. It'll just encourage copycats, like "BLT," who kills you and then has a nice sandwich. Or "KFC," who kills you and then places your body parts in a bucket. Or "ADD," who starts killing you but then loses interest. Or "LBJ," who kills you while holding you up by the ears. Or RSVP, who plans to kill you, but then calls and says he can't make it . . .

Hooked on Ebonics

NEW RULE

Cut the shnizzle. We all know it's hilarious when white people—especially old ladies—talk "street" on TV, but early reports indicate that every single network sitcom this season will feature at least one 8-year-old kid saying "shnizzle." Attention all real rappers—you have guns for a reason. Use them.

Hysterical Blandness

NEW RULE

Don't type "lol" unless you really "laugh out loud." Many Web chatters have picked up the annoying habit of typing "lol" after just about everything you say. "How are you?" "lol" "The pope died." "lol" "I slowly peel back the waistband of my cottony-white briefs, unleashing my fully erect 9-inch pole." "lol" Look, if I wanted a kiss-ass session where every thought I utter gets a big, phony laugh, I'd call a meeting with my writers.

Flee Circus

NEW RULE

Don't say a woman is crazy just because she runs away from her wedding. She'd be crazy if she wanted to spend the rest of her life servicing this goober.

When I heard the news that a young bride-to-be had gone missing on a jog days before her wedding, I had the same thought everyone else did: Man, that Scott Peterson is *good*.

Americans reacted to the so-called runaway bride by branding her as crazy for skipping town rather than marrying a Sunday school teacher in Duluth, Georgia. Ah, yes, the good life—the bake sales, the prayer meetings, the abortion protests—who could just walk away from all that? How come when the girl from *Titanic* ditches her fiancé, it's the greatest romance of all time, but when Jennifer Wilbanks does it, she's a criminal loon with a case of temporary insanity? Temporary sanity is more like it. She was staring down the barrel of 14 bridesmaids and 600 guests in the Georgia heat watching a Baptist in a blue suit sanctify her sex life with Welch's Grape Juice and a reading from *The Purpose Driven Life*—suddenly Greyhound to Vegas looked pretty good.

Jennifer, I applaud your rugged individualism. You eloped with yourself. And to Vegas, baby—that's money. I mean, what happens in Vegas stays in Vegas, whereas the woman who marries in Georgia . . . stays in Georgia.

Jen, you're a free spirit, I can tell. Something inside you snapped and rebelled at the idea of living in a persistent vegetative state—which is why tonight I'd like to offer you an open invitation to come out here. We'll even send you the $118 dollar bus ticket—first class, right behind the driver.

Come on! Come all the way over to the dark side. You can stay in my hot tub till you get back on your feet. You're crazy and you don't care about anyone's feelings but your own—you belong in Hollywood. You're a reality show waiting to happen. Plus there are a lot of eligible bachelors here. Pat O'Brien's available. I can introduce you. And I've got some stuff that you can smoke that might alleviate some of that pressure behind your eyeballs. And don't worry about that fiancé of yours. Believe me, by the time I'm finished with you, he won't want you back.

I Do-Wop

NEW RULE

There's nothing wrong with being a little old bald guy and marrying a 23-year-old. That's why God created money. Stop talking about how embarrassing Billy Joel's marriage is. Driving into every tree in East Hampton? That's embarrassing. "We Didn't Start the Fire"? *Embarrassing.* This is the first thing he's done since "The Stranger" that makes perfect sense.

I Hear Dead People

NEW RULE

If you find a new record from anyone dead, it sucks. If Elvis or Tupac or Kurt Cobain thought they had a hit, they would have released it back when it could have helped them get blown.

Chicken Hawk Down

NEW RULE

The people in America who were most in favor of the Iraq war must go there and fight it. The army missed its recruiting goal by 42 percent a few months ago—more people joined the Michael Jackson Fan Club. We've done picked all the low-lying Lynndie England fruit, and now we need warm bodies. We need warm bodies like Paula Abdul needs . . . warm bodies.

A Baptist Minister in North Carolina told nine members of his congregation that unless they renounced their 2004 vote for John Kerry, they had to leave his church. Well—if we're *that* certain these days that George Bush is always *that* right about everything, then going to Iraq to fulfill the glorious leader's vision would seem the least one could do.

Hey, if it makes it any easier, just think of it as a reality show. *Fear Factor: Shitting Your Pants Edition. Survivor: Sunni Triangle.* Or maybe a video game: Grand Theft Allah.

I know, you're thinking, "But Bill, I already do my part with the 'Support Our Troops' magnet I have on my Chevy Tahoe—how much more can one man give?"

Here's an intriguing economic indicator: It's been over a year since they graduated, but neither of the Bush twins has been able to find work. Why don't they sign up for Iraq duty? Do they hate America or just freedom in general?

I Promise I'll Be Yentl

NEW RULE

Jewish people have to start having sex. The Jewish population in America dropped 5 percent in the last decade, which may explain why this country's finances have gone to shit. Breed, you sons of Abraham—breed! We need you. Israel needs you. Kobe Bryant, Robert Blake, and Phil Spector need you. Plus, without Jews, who's going to write all those sitcoms about blacks and Hispanics?

That goes for everybody who helped sell this war—you gotta go first. Brooks and Dunn? Drop your cocks and grab your socks. Ann Coulter: Darling, trust me, you will love the army. You think *you* make up stuff? Curt Schilling? Bye-bye. You ended the curse on Boston? Good. Let's try your luck on Fallujah. Oh, and that Republican Baldwin brother has to go, too, so that Ted Nugent has someone to frag.

But mostly, we have to send Mr. and Mrs. Britney Spears, because Britney once said: " . . . we should trust our president in every decision that he makes, and we should just support that and be faithful in what happens."

Somebody has to die for that. Hell, Britney's already knocked up, so that'll save the guards at Abu Ghraib about 10 minutes. And think of the spiritual lift it will provide to troops and civilians alike when actual combat smacks the smirk off of Kevin Federline's face and fills his low-hanging trousers with duty.

In summation, you can't advocate for something you wouldn't do yourself. For example, I'm for fuel efficiency, which is why I drive a hybrid car and always take an electric private plane. I'm for legalizing marijuana, so I smoke a ton of it. And I'm for gay marriage, which is why—oh well, you get the point.

Inky Dinky Don't

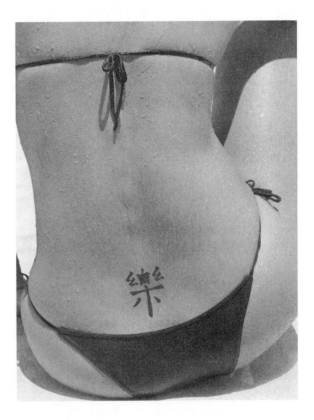

NEW RULE

Just because your tattoo has Chinese characters in it, it doesn't make you spiritual. It's right above the crack of your ass and it translates to "Beef with Broccoli." The last time you did anything spiritual, you were praying to God you weren't pregnant.

Inside the Actors' Ego

NEW RULE

Stop calling acting a "craft." What witches do is a craft. Those wallets that head-injury patients make are a craft. What you do is make us believe what isn't so. You're, you're . . . a two-faced liar. And if you're going to hand out awards for that, why snub the masters?

Internet Virus

NEW RULE

You can't notify people by e-mail that you've given them chlamydia. The San Francisco Health Department has a new service that lets you send an Internet greeting card to someone you may have infected with an STD: "Roses are red, orchids are gray, congratulations, you have hepatitis A."

It's Dead, Jim

NEW RULE

Let TV shows die a natural death. Fans of the cancelled TV series *Star Trek: Enterprise* are trying to raise enough money on their own to pay for another season. It's either that or go outside. So far they've raised $3 million, largely by not dating. Hey, Trekkies, if you really want to donate money to a lost cause, try MoveOn.org.

Sin-a-Plex

NEW RULE

There's no such thing as Hollywood values. In honor of the Oscars, let me just say that every time I see some pundit say Hollywood is out of touch, I just want to take my big screen plasma TV, march it right down to the end of my private road, and throw it over the big iron gate!

"Hollywood versus America" is a tactic that works well as conservative red meat, a continuation of the "Red State vs. Blue State" theme of the last election, where blue staters were convinced everything between New York and L.A. was one giant forest where Ned Beatty is constantly being sodomized by hillbillies, and red staters were told that people like me spend all our time performing abortions and figuring out new ways to desecrate the flag. Please, they're just hobbies.

Politically, it's always been advantageous to divide people—to make America a place of warmongers versus wimps, elitists versus morons, gun nuts versus people with normal-size penises. Only problem is, it's not true. Hollywood isn't your cesspool, America; it's your mirror. We made all those movies with the smirking sex and the mindless violence and the superheroes beating the shit out of zombies because that's what you wanted.

It's what the whole world wants. Movies are the one thing about America the rest of the world still actually likes—America's last export. I mean besides the torture. And even the ones being tortured are like, "Cool, this is just like in *The Deer Hunter*."

So to those who think that if we just put *Leave It to Beaver* back on, the gay people would come to their senses, I say this: Stop worrying. Hollywood won't turn your daughter into a nymphomaniac or get her hooked on drugs. I will. And she'll still be better for it—because I'll teach her that there's more to values than reciting things, praying, and voting for Bush, that being moral actually involves making choices guided by principles like fairness and tolerance.

For example, there was a woman in Alaska who cut off her husband's penis and flushed it down the toilet. Based on that, I would agree, our morality is in decline, because 10 years ago, when Lorena Bobbitt cut off her husband's penis, she didn't flush it down the toilet, where it *could* never be retrieved. She threw it out the window of a moving car, where it could be retrieved and was. So, come on, America, admit it: When it comes to Hollywood, you love us, you really love us!

BILL MAHER

NEW RULES

Jersey, Sure

NEW RULE

Let the Mafia protect New Jersey. Terror experts say that the deadliest, most vulnerable 2 miles in America is the unguarded chemical corridor in New Jersey that gave the state its reputation for smelling like a sweat sock. Arizona has the Minute Men; let New Jersey have the Mafia. They all live there anyway.

Jet Blew

NEW RULE

After the plane lands, airlines must stop saying, "Thank you for choosing us." There is no choosing anymore. I took the only flight that left within 8 hours of when I wanted to go, by the only airline that went there. Nobody chooses Southwest—Southwest chooses you. If I need to be in Spokane, Washington, by tomorrow morning, I either take the flight I'm given, or I mail myself in a Fed-Ex box.

Ji-Hard

NEW RULE

If we really want to stop terrorism, we have to get Muslim men laid. Five British Muslims who were recently sent home from our prison at Guantanamo accused their American captors of bringing in prostitutes to taunt them. It turned out that most of them had never even seen a woman naked before. This naturally made me wonder how many members of al-Qaeda have ever even dated a girl and what would happen if we hired women to infiltrate al-Qaeda cells and have sex with them.

I'll bet you things would change quickly after this covert operation. Because young Muslim men don't really hate America—they're jealous of America. We have rap videos, the Hilton sisters, and magazines with titles like *Barely Legal*. You know what's barely legal in Afghanistan? *Everything.*

Young men need sex, and if they don't get it for months on end, they wind up cursing the day they ever decided to go to Cornell.

Have you ever wondered why the word from the "Arab street" is so angry? It's because it's a bunch of guys standing in the street! Which is what guys do when they don't have girlfriends; when they're not allowed to even talk to a girl. Of course they want to commit suicide—unlike in this country, where it's the married guys who wanna kill themselves.

But here, there's always hope that if you can at least talk to a girl, she might be crazy enough to go for you. Or you could get rich and buy one, like people do in Beverly Hills.

The connection between no sex and anger is real. It's why prizefighters stay celibate when they're in training: so that on fight night, they're pissed off and ready to kill. It's why football players don't have sex after Wednesday. And, conversely, it's why Bill Clinton never started a war.

So to paraphrase the sign in his old war room: It's the pussy, stupid. We need the Coalition of the Willing to be *really* willing. We need to mobilize two divisions of skanks, a regiment of hos, and a brigade of girls who just can't say no—all under the command of Colonel Ann Coulter, who'll be dressed in her "Ilsa, She-Wolf of the S.S." uniform.

Forget the Peace Corps; we need a Piece-of-Ass Corps. Girls, there's a cure for terrorism, and you're sitting on it.

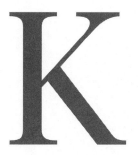

K-9 Jelly

NEW RULE

Gay marriage won't lead to dog marriage. It is not a slippery slope to rampant interspecies coupling. When women got the right to vote, it didn't lead to hamsters voting. No court has extended the equal protection clause to salmon. And for the record, all marriages are "same sex" marriages. You get married, and every night, it's the same sex.

Krystal Not

NEW RULE

Stop saying anybody or anything is like the Nazis. Republicans aren't like the Nazis. Neo-Nazis aren't even like the Nazis. Nothing is like the Nazis. Except for Wal-Mart.

Kidiots

NEW RULE

Leave the children behind. Leave them behind at least until they've learned something. A new survey finds that only half of America's high schoolers think newspapers should be allowed to publish without government approval, and almost one in five said Americans should be prohibited from expressing unpopular opinions. Lemme tell you little darlings something: This is my livelihood you're screwing with now, so learn the Bill of Rights, or you don't deserve Social Security.

Now, to those of you who think I'm overreacting here, yes, I understand that when you are in high school you are still very young and no one really cares what kids say anyway—after all, it's not like priests are dating them for their brains. But the younger generation is supposed to rage against the machine, not for it; they're supposed to question authority, not question those who question authority—and what's so frightening here is that we're seeing the beginnings of the first post 9/11 generation, kids who first became aware of the news under an "Americans need to watch what they say" administration, kids who've been told that dissent is un-American and therefore justifiably punished by fine, imprisonment, or loss of your show on ABC.

President Bush once posed the question "Is our children learning?" No, President Bush—they isn't. And so a more appropriate question might be "Is our teachers teaching?" In 4 years, you can teach a gorilla sign language—is it too much to ask that in the same amount of time, a teenager in America be taught what those crazy hippies who founded this country had in mind?

I know the Morals & Values folks want us to take time out of every school day for praying, memorizing the Ten Commandments, abstinence training, and learning at least two theories of evolution (the one agreed upon by every scientist in the world and also the one involving a naked lady and a snake)—but lest we forget, the people of Iraq risked death and danger to send us one simple, inspiring message: America, get out of our country. But also, we want the freedoms you take for granted.

I didn't mind being on the losing side of the last election, but as a loser, I guess I have some "unpopular" opinions—and, if you don't mind, I'd like to keep them. I'd even like to say them right out loud on TV, because if I just sit here every Friday night and spout Bush administration–approved talking points, that's not freedom or entertainment. It's Fox News.

Hitting below the Beltway

NEW RULE

You can't be a Washington outsider if you're already the president. Hearing President Bush constantly complain about "the politicians" and the "Washington mind-set" and saying things like "I got news for the Washington crowd" is like hearing Courtney Love bitch about junkies.

"Washington Insider" is by definition a function of one's proximity to the president. That's you, Mr. Bush. When you're given check-writing privileges by the Federal Reserve, you just might be a Washington Insider.

Put it this way: You're not the Mr. Smith in *Mr. Smith Goes to Washington*— you're the Washington part. We need a Mr. Smith to fuck with *you*! You're not on a mission you reluctantly accepted, like the old farts in *Space Cowboys*—you campaigned for it. So it's a little late to be selling yourself as some fish-out-of-water cowboy visiting the big city on assignment. You're not Mc-Cloud. For 17 of the last 24 years you've had a key to the White House. The last thing that happened in Washington without you Bushes getting a piece was Marion Barry's crack habit. *The Exorcist* happened in Georgetown, but Satan had to run it by Jim Baker first.

Lassie, Stay Home

NEW RULE

No more dog shows. Prodding and grooming and training an innocent animal to fit some arbitrary human definition of perfection is abuse, plain and simple. There's only one proper way to show a dog she's adored—ask her to marry you.

Last Writes

NEW RULE

You can't write your own obituary. There's this hot new trend now: writing your own death notice before you die. It's a nice new way of saying "I may be dead, but I can still monopolize the conversation." You're dead. Worms are eating you. Let someone else talk.

Law and Order: SUV

NEW RULE

You might think this one is self-evident, but: Don't watch TV when you drive. A man is on trial for a fatal crash that happened while he was driving and watching *Road Trip*. A moving automobile isn't a theater. It's a place for eating, drinking, talking on the phone, doing your hair, checking your makeup, and getting blown.

Lemon Law

NEW RULE

I don't need an annoying little sticker on each individual piece of fruit. Let me get this straight: Our borders aren't secure, but we're still going through the plums by hand? The stickers are the opposite of appetizing—especially the ones on kiwis that say, "Don't these things kind of look like your balls?"

Let Freedom Jiggle

N E W   R U L E

Lap dancing is a First Amendment right. The L.A. city council has banned lap dancing. What's next—burning books? Lap dancers, or "imagineers," as I like to call them, are artists, drawing you into their fantasy world much like a skilled novelist does—that is, if novelists had perfectly waxed bikini lines. But more important, lap dancers are expressing an idea—an idea called hope: the hope that someday, a skinny young woman with artificial breasts and a navel piercing will want to have sex with you. And without that hope, millions of American men might just as well throw themselves into the sea.

Lipstick Thespians

NEW RULE

Go back to calling actresses actresses, not actors. Every word we say doesn't have to be gender neutral. And by the way, it's not a hate crime to say that Madonna is a bad actress, not a bad actor.

Lite Remark

NEW RULE

Having "no carbs" doesn't necessarily make something good. This New Rule has no carbs and it's not funny.

Lost Verizon

NEW RULE

I don't need my cell phone to play video games or access the Internet or double as a walkie-talkie—I just need it to make a phone call. Why is getting to level four of Tomb Raider no problem but to have a simple conversation I have to stand on a hilltop with my nuts wrapped in tinfoil? When it comes to cell phones, I just need the basics: something that rings at inappropriate moments, interferes with airplane safety, and gives me a brain tumor.

Love Thy Neighbor

NEW RULE

Don't try to talk to me about *Desperate Housewives*. If I had the slightest interest in other people's sex lives, I'd be a Republican.

Super Bull

NEW RULE

The Super Bowl must stop pretending it doesn't take advocacy ads. In turning down ads from certain charities like PETA, CBS and the NFL claim they don't accept advocacy ads, which is ridiculous because every Super Bowl ad is an advocacy ad, and what they mostly advocate is eating fried food and drinking beer until you explode.

Not that they care if you die from food, because death by eating is always acceptable in America. Apparently death by fucking is a different matter. There was a watch-out-for-AIDS ad during the last pregame, which is all well and good, except AIDS doesn't even place in the Top 15 of the things that kill people in this country—but what does place all over that list is food and drink: Almost twice as many Americans die from liver disease as from AIDS. Where's the Super Bowl ad with a *Will and Grace* cast member telling us to pull a condom over our Bud Light bottle?

Four times as many die of diabetes versus AIDS; 47 times as many from heart disease. We're kidding ourselves to think it's not the toxicity in our food supply that's doing us in. The nutritional guide at KFC is a card that reads "You're kidding me, right?" Guys watch the Super Bowl while eating an entire tub of guacamole and then announce, "Hey, it's the good kind of fat." No, the good kind of fat is J.Lo's ass.

And I'll have no part of the argument that McDonald's and Fritos prevent AIDS because they make you so fat, nobody wants to have sex with you. You can't even sell sex anymore without making it sound like food. How do you think they came up with "booty-licious?"

Speaking of which, you know who else is sponsoring the Super Bowl? Levitra, Viagra, and Cialis. No, those aren't three black chicks I know—okay, they are—but they're also the names of three boner pills, because let's face it: What every woman in America wants on Super Bowl Sunday evening is a gassy, flabby, face-painted drunk coming after her with a raging hard-on.

Name Dropping

NEW RULE

Stop leaving messages on my answering machine saying "It's me." I already have a "me" in my life—me. And, frankly, if we were that close, I'd have given you the number of the phone that I answer.

Navy Seals

NEW RULE

No exploiting animals for the war effort. The military is using trained dolphins and sea lions to root out underwater mines. I remember when balancing balls on your nose got you kicked *out* of the Navy.

Newsweak

NEW RULE

News organizations have to stop using the phrase "We go beyond the head-lines." That's your job, dummy. You don't see American Airlines saying "We land our jets on the runway!"

No Big Thing

NEW RULE

When the penis-enlargement pills you bought fail to enlarge your penis, don't file a lawsuit. Yes, I'm talking to you, Michael Coluzzi of Burlington, New Jersey. You see, Michael Coluzzi, lawsuits are in the public record and now everyone in Burlington knows you, Michael Coluzzi, have a shameful secret.

No-Coin-Do

NEW RULE

Tipping is for waiters, bathroom attendants, and lap dancers only! What is it with Starbucks, delis, even dry cleaners, all having little jars on the counter? Hmm, what's 15 percent of "blow me"? Waiters get tips because they wait on you. If your job involves standing behind a counter cutting bagels in half, you're not waiting on me—I'm waiting on you!

No Free Crunch

NEW RULE

Homeless shelters don't need gyms. Los Angeles just opened a new homeless shelter with a library, hair salon, and gym. Now, I'm fine with the library and the hair salon—like most people, I like my crack whores well read and groomed—but a gym? If you're pushing a loaded shopping cart around all day, you don't need a StairMaster. I know gay guys who became homeless just for the abs.

Nookie Monster

NEW RULE

No puppet fucking. The movie *Team America* features graphic sex scenes between marionettes. If I had any interest in wooden sex with strings attached, I'd get married.

The Crying Games

NEW RULE

One of the guy networks like ESPN has to broadcast an old-school version of the Olympics that leaves out all the "Hallmark moments" and just shows sports.

Adolf Hitler once used the Olympics to demonstrate that Aryans were strong; NBC uses them to show the world that Americans like to cry a lot. Look, I understand that everything nowadays has to be rendered bloated, syrupy, dumbed down, and sentimental—this is America, after all. But for those of you out there who may be too young to remember a time before Oprah ruined everything: In the old days when we watched the Olympics, it wasn't continuous sob-sister profiles interrupted by the occasional sporting event—it was just the events. There was none of this stuff about the heartbreak and pain it took to become the best damn kayaker a man can be. It was enough just to watch a man throw a long stick or a big iron ball. His mom's chemotherapy, his sister's glass eye, and his dog, a wounded combat vet—they never entered into it. We weren't told whose grandpa was paralyzed in a tractor accident or that the decathlon guy has a cleft palate and overcame a lifetime of bed-wetting to go for the gold, because if someone had told us that, we would have said, "Hey, if I wanted to sit through hours of melodramatic personal backstory, I'd pay attention to my date."

Take Nancy Pitts of the US women's wrestling team. Two years ago, the unthinkable happened to Nancy—she was diagnosed with prostate cancer. Happily, it was caught in time, and she was able to go back to her usual training regimen: 3 hours of weight lifting, followed by an hour of shaving.

Somehow the press now gives the Olympics the sort of coverage once reserved for a war, though actual wars are treated like sporting events. NBC aired 1,200 hours of Olympic coverage, 400 times more than they gave the Democratic convention, but what the heck, that was just about war and peace in the nuclear age—the Olympics are about swimming. Oh, if only they were! If only we could get the swimming without the three-hankie immigrant parents, the latchkey kids, the single moms, and all the brave athletes who rose before dawn and traveled hours in the frosty silence of the Iowa winter just to meet their drug dealers.

The Olympic Games are that rarest of events, a coalition of a great variety of nations coming together for a purpose other than killing Iraqis. So please, media barons, just give us one channel where it's simply about the competition and the belief that how high a man can hop is also a measure of who has the best country.

And this way you can keep the focus-group–approved drivel disguised as in-depth analysis where it belongs: in the coverage of presidential elections.

BILL MAHER

NEW RULES

Only Begotten Sony

NEW RULE

If you have to set up a big-screen TV and show the Daytona 500 to get people into your church, as one church in Fredericksburg, Virginia, does, then your flock is not worshipping Jesus; they're worshipping Dale Earnhardt Jr. And there's a difference: One is the son of god, and the other died on a cross for your sins.

Ooh la Lame

NEW RULE

Someone must stop the Cirque du Soleil. If we hate the French so much, how come we gave them Las Vegas? There are now six Cirque du Soleil–related shows on the Strip. Six! Who wants to spend 2 hours watching a bunch of French chicks fold themselves in half? You know what, scratch that. New Rule: We need more Cirque du Soleil.

Operation Dessert Storm

NEW RULE

Ice cream should stay nonpartisan. Some right-wingers started an ice cream company to counteract the lefties at Ben & Jerry's with flavors like I Hate the French Vanilla, Iraqi Road, and Smaller Govern-Mint. I know, I know, anything to get Ann Coulter to eat. But they're missing the whole point of Ben & Jerry's—hippie ice cream is fun because you eat it when you're stoned.

Osama Been Hidin'

NEW RULE

The president must stop saying that Osama Bin Laden "can run but he can't hide." Boy, can he hide. We can't find him with cruise missiles, satellites, or million-dollar bribes—although, oddly enough, he is reachable through Classmates.com.

Oscar Nod

NEW RULE

The Oscar broadcast must come in at some time under 6 hours. The Oscars are like having sex with someone on coke: It all starts out very exciting but, several hours in, you really just want them to finish.

Taint Misbehavin'

NEW RULE

Abstinence pledges make you horny. In a setback for the morals/values crowd, a new 8-year study reveals that American teenagers who take "virginity" pledges wind up with just as many STDs as the other kids do. But that's not all—taking the pledge also makes a teenage girl six times more likely to perform oral sex and four times more likely to allow anal. Which leads me to an important question: Where were these pledges when I was in high school?

Seriously, when I was a teenager, the only kids having anal intercourse were the ones who missed. My idea of lubrication was oiling my bike chain. If I had known I could have been getting porn-star sex the same year I took Algebra II simply by joining up with the Christian Right, I'd have been so down with Jesus, they would have had to pry me out of the pew.

There are a lot worse things than teenagers having sex—namely, teenagers *not* having sex. Here's something you'll never hear: "That suicide bomber blew himself up because he was having too much sex. Sex, sex, sex, nonstop. All that crazy Arab ever had was sex, and look what happened."

The theory of the puritans of the 21st century seems to be: The less kids

know about sex, the better. Because people who talk about pee-pees are potty mouths. And so armed with limited knowledge and believing regular vaginal intercourse to be either immaculate or filthy dirty, these kids did with their pledge what everybody does with contracts: They found loopholes—two of them, to be exact.

Is there any greater irony than the fact that the Christian Right actually got their precious little adolescent daughters to say to their freshly scrubbed boyfriends: "Please, I want to remain pure for my wedding night, so only in the ass. Then I'll blow you." Well, at least these kids are really thinking outside the box.

Pasta la Vista

NEW RULE

If you're in Iraq and you even sort of think you might be kind of near a checkpoint . . . stop. Otherwise, don't be surprised if we shoot your car. Haven't you seen a single American movie, television show, or news story from the last 60 years? That's what we do: We shoot cars. Does the name Elvis ring a bell? Richard Pryor? Lee Harvey Oswald? I know it's hard for foreigners to understand, but in America we shoot first and ask questions rarely.

Pay Ball!

NEW RULE

Stop saying that athletes do it for the love of the game. They do it for the love of their 32-room mansion with the live shark tank in the living room. Bass fishermen do it for the love of the game, which is why so few of them have agents. If pro sports paid minimum wage, Shaquille O'Neal would be a bouncer at Scores, and Anna Kournikova would be a mail-order bride from Minsk.

Pewsweek

NEW RULE

Time Magazine has to change its name to *God Weekly*. In the last few years, Time has put out: "The Secrets of the Nativity," "The God Gene," "Faith, God and the Oval Office," "The Bible and the Apocalypse," "Who Was Moses?" "What Jesus Saw," "Why Did Jesus Have to Die?" "Jesus at 2000." If Jesus gets any more free press, he's going to start thinking he's Paris Hilton. Look, I understand we have a lot of Christians in this nation, but how about a little equal time?

"Vishnu to Ganesh: 'Drop Dead!'" and "Is There No Pleasing Zeus?"

Pie-Curious

NEW RULE

Homosexuals must be ripped. As news reports covered gay couples marrying in 2004, America was forced to confront a real eye-opener: A gay person can be just as big a slob as a straight one. We saw couples with beer guts and 9-day-old stubble, wearing hockey jerseys. And I don't just mean the lesbians. Guys, I know you're new at this matrimony thing, but this is how it works: First you get married, *then* you let yourself go.

Pitt Happens

NEW RULE

Let the two best-looking people in the world have sex with each other. We all knew they'd end up together—we've been to high school. He was just waiting a respectable interval for her to shed that Billy Bob smell.

Pluck Off

N E W R U L E

Ladies, leave your eyebrows alone. Here's how much men care about your eyebrows: Do you have two of them? Okay, we're done.

Pontiff-icating

N E W R U L E

Don't get movie blurbs from the pope, like the pontiff's famous "It is as it was" rave for Mel Gibson's Jesus movie. What he really said was:

"James Caviezel is Christ-errific!"

"Monica Belluci puts the mmm! in Mary Magdalene!"

"She could wash my feet anytime!"

"A rock-hard 10 on the St. Peter Meter!"

Pope Goes Caviezel

NEW RULE

Stop asking Jim Caviezel religious questions. He just played Jesus in a movie. It's like asking a cast member of *Scrubs* to lance a boil. Why, if everyone on TV was really like the character he plays, no one at church would talk to me, my wife, or my eight kids.

Bi-Definition

NEW RULE

You can't claim you're the party of smaller government and then make laws about love. What business is it of the state how consenting adults choose to pair off, share expenses, and eventually stop having sex with each other?

Why does the Bush administration want a constitutional amendment about weddings? Hey, why stop at weddings—birthdays are important; let's put them in the great document. Let's make a law that gay people can have birthdays, but straight people get more cake—you know, to send the right message to kids.

Republicans are always saying we should privatize things, like schools, prison, social security—how about we privatize privacy? If the government forbids gay men from tying the knot, what's their alternative? They can't all marry Liza Minelli.

Republicans used to be the party that opposed social engineering, but now they push programs to outlaw marriage for some people and encourage it for others. If you're straight, there's a billion-five in the budget to promote marriage, but gay marriage is opposed because it threatens or mocks—or does something—to the "sanctity of marriage," as if anything you can do in Vegas drunk off your ass in front of an Elvis impersonator could be considered sacred.

Half the people who pledge eternal love are doing it because one of them is either knocked up, rich, or desperate. But, in George Bush's mind, marriage is a beautiful lifetime bond of love and sharing—kind of like what he has with the Saudis.

But at least the Right isn't hypocritical on this issue; they really believe that homosexuality is an "abomination" and a dysfunction that's "curable." They also believe that if a gay man just devotes his life to Jesus, he'll stop being gay—because that theory worked out so well with the Catholic priests.

But the greater shame in this story goes to the Democrats. They don't believe homosexuality is an abomination, and therefore their refusal to en-

So-Duh

NEW RULE

There's no such thing as "flavored water." There's a whole aisle of this crap at the supermarket—water, but without the watery taste. Sorry, but flavored water is called a soft drink. You want flavored water? Pour some scotch over ice and let it melt. That's your flavored water.

Softening Dick

NEW RULE

Keep Dick Cheney in seclusion. I liked it better when the vice president was always tucked away in an undisclosed location. He's like the creature in the cradle at the end of *Rosemary's Baby*: It's more frightening when all we see is the rattle in its horrible little hand. Stick to your original strategy: Only bring out Dick Cheney when you're trying to make Rumsfeld seem human.

Sour Kraut

NEW RULE

"Eat me" is just an expression. Another German man has been convicted of killing and eating someone, the second such case in a year. You can always tell a German cannibal because he says things like "I'm so hungry I could eat a Horst."

Square Dunce

NEW RULE

Country music stars can't be authors. Charlie Daniels's book *Ain't No Rag: Freedom, Family, and the Flag* is a collection of musings by noted white trash icon Charlie Daniels on subjects ranging from American flags to American flag bumper stickers to what to do to a hippie if you catch him trying to burn an American flag. Before this book, I was ambivalent on the issue of flag burning. Now, I find myself reconsidering the question of book burning.

Star Bores

NEW RULE

No more referring to your acting role as "this wonderful journey." It wasn't a journey. You just mixed the wrong pills in your trailer and then went to the set and acted like someone slightly less fucked up than you.

Statue of Limitations

NEW RULE

Keep the Statue of Liberty closed. Since 9/11, the statue has been off limits for security reasons, and some people are outraged. Why? It's a sacred symbol of our principles, not a StairMaster. Everything doesn't have to be interactive. People go to church; they don't take turns up on the cross. You're not allowed to fill the Liberty Bell with nachos or wear it as a hat. You want to lose yourself inside an American icon? Have sex with Shelley Winters.

Statuette of Limitations

NEW RULE

Best sound editing is not a category at the Oscars. Ditto sound mixing. Talkies have been around for 70 years. Hollywood, you nailed the sound thing. The only part that matters about movie sound is that it's really, really loud. Otherwise, I'll be able to think, and if I think, I'll realize I'm a college-educated adult watching a movie about a Spiderman.

Stiff Up Her Lip

NEW RULE

There's no explaining love. If Charles and Camilla prove one thing, it's that she must be the greatest lay in history. She must do things to him that make Carmen Elektra look like your hand. Love is inexplicable, so let's not put any laws about marriage in our Constitution.

Storm Frontin'

NEW RULE

Hurricane names should be scary. It's bad enough we can't name hurricanes after women anymore because it's sexist; now they're all getting Waspy names like "Alex," which is the least effective approach. Can you imagine how much faster the Carolinas would evacuate if they announced that "Ludacris" was headed their way?

Orifice Politics

NEW RULE

Fucking around at the office is not a reason to lose your job. If it was, the unemployment rate in America would be 80 percent. You may have heard that the CEO of Boeing—or as it's now known, Boing!—had to step down because he was having an affair with the nice lady from accounts receivable. Who gives a damn?

I know what you're saying: "Hey Bill, that attitude may be fine for you, leading your 'single, libertarian lifestyle'—but when a 68-year-old airline executive named Harry Stonecipher bones somebody in the supply closet, what do we tell the children?"

Right, "the children," who look up to geriatric arms dealers and obviously don't want to think of their government buying Apache helicopters from a fornicator. "At Boeing, we will not tolerate sneaking around! Now get back to work on the Stealth bomber."

In other countries, a CEO committing adultery isn't even called a "scandal." It's called a "business trip." Why are there so many puritans in this country, and why can't the rest of us make them go away? When did we get to be such a nation of busybodies? Oooh, who's Harry Stonecipher fucking? I gotta know.

Just to put things into perspective, Boeing Company is our second largest defense contractor. They make things like the F-15, and we're at war, with soldiers' lives at stake, so I gotta think the smooth, uninterrupted management of the Boeing Company might be important—but apparently not more important than stopping Harry Stonecipher from grappling naked in a burlesque of lust with 52-year-old Gloria Hormth.

Not long ago, we found out there's nine billion of our dollars missing in Iraq—not misspent: lost. You heard me: $9 billion. But in the age of Bush, anything that involves money is legal, and the only scandal is sex. Gross, disgusting, AARP, early-bird-special sex with Harry Stonecipher. As if a 68-year-old man having an office romance should be a shock in the aerospace industry—it shouldn't; it should be a high five in the pharmaceutical industry. This sort of event shouldn't be condemned; it should be applauded. Harry Stonecipher's extramarital affair is the first time Boeing ever deployed an obsolete missile system and you and I didn't have to foot the bill for it.

BILL MAHER

NEW RULES

Tallowed Be Thy Name

NEW RULE

Jesus is not a candle. A company in South Dakota is selling candles with the scent of Jesus. You light one, and your friends say, "Christ, what's that smell?" It's true, the formula comes straight out of the Bible—it's from the little-known Letter of Paul to the Aromatherapists. But if Jesus really smelled so great, how come everybody was always offering to wash his feet?

Tart Reform

First Amber Frey was mad that Scott Peterson was married. Then she was mad that he had killed his wife.

NEW RULE

There's just no pleasing some people.

1040 BS

NEW RULE

That computer setup in your home where you play video golf at night and your wife has sexy cyber chats with strangers during the day is not a tax-deductible "in-home office." It's a chair in your family room, facing away from your family.

The Book of Moron

NEW RULE

If Utah gets to edit Hollywood, then Hollywood gets to edit Utah. Four Utah-based companies are taking popular movies, editing out parts they don't like, and then selling them to other sexually repressed squares. Let me ask you this, Spencer: How'd you like it if we went through the Book of Mormon and took out all the bullshit? You have your fantasy world—it involves celestial marriage and magic underpants—and we have ours: It involves Sin City and a half-naked Jessica Alba. Instead of asking yourself "What would Jesus edit?" accept that maybe *Pooty Tang* just isn't for you. You don't see me adding jokes to Pauly Shore movies. Believe me, it won't up your street cred when you bring home *Dude, Where's My Bible?*

The Guest Wing

NEW RULE

The president can have sleepovers. It turns out President Bush puts up some of his big-name donors in the Lincoln bedroom just like Clinton! And you know what? I still don't care. If Bush wants to get in his footy pajamas and have CEOs over to play Battleship, fine. If that's all Bush donors are getting for their money, it's not called "a scandal"—it's called "a good start."

The L-Word

NEW RULE

Stop saying tax-and-spend liberal. That's what the government does: It taxes and spends. As opposed to the system under Bush/Cheney: Dine-and-dash.

Three Reichs and You're Out

NEW RULE

George Bush isn't Hitler. In the 2004 election, MoveOn.org compared Bush to Hitler, ignoring the first rule for being taken seriously by grown-ups, which is: Don't call everyone you don't like "Hitler." Bush is not Hitler. For one thing, Hitler was a decorated, frontline combat veteran. Also, in the election that brought him to power in 1933, Hitler got more votes than the other candidates.

And Hitler had a mustache. So let's all take a rest from playing the Hitler card. Unless we're talking about Saddam Hussein. Now, that guy was Hitler.

Tiara Alert

NEW RULE

No more "talent competitions" at beauty pageants. Being hot *is* a talent. The only reason we endured watching Miss Texas play the xylophone in the first place was because it made her breasts jiggle. The talent contest is just an interminable delay to the whole point of the night: getting date-raped by an athlete.

Till Debt Do Us Part

NEW RULE

Enough with the bitching about the credit card companies. Sure, they're a bunch of predatory loan sharks, but your credit problems may also have something to do with the fact that you just can't stop buying stuff. So, set down your $5, double-mocha, no-foam latte and your plasma-screen, Internet-accessible, camera cell phone and face the fact that there's only one surefire way to erase credit card debt—by picking up a big, shiny pair of scissors . . . and cutting your wife in half.

Tit for Tat

NEW RULE

No breast-feeding in public. Some women think it's okay to openly breast-feed in the restaurant while I'm trying to eat. They say it's healthy and natural. Well, so is my date's libido—but you don't see her blowing me next to the dessert cart.

AND NEW RULE

You can't choose to be a cheap whore at only one specific place and time. If you show your breasts for plastic beads at Mardi Gras in New Orleans, then you have to show your breasts for beads at a Houlihan's in Philadelphia.

To Kill a Sunrise

NEW RULE

"Morning people" must keep it to themselves. By the time you stop and explain that you're a morning person, it's too late—you've already annoyed me. We get it—you're up and ready to go at the crack of dawn, just like my dick.

Pique Performance

NEW RULE

Republicans need anger management training. I talk to young people all the time, and over and over again, they have the same complaint: that I'm out of Schnapps. But their other big gripe is that there's really no difference between the two parties. Not true: The Republicans are much more pissed off. Look at John Bolton—if you can. Now, I don't know if this man has human relationship issues, but I do know two things: One, his hair's not speaking to his mustache. And two, The Republicans actually like the idea of our most sensitive diplomatic post being helmed by a raging psychopath. Asking John Bolton to represent you at the UN is like asking R. Kelly to chaperone the Miss Teen USA Pageant—you know someone's gonna end up pissed.

Like Mr. Bolton, what Republicans need is to find a channel for their anger; I mean a channel besides Fox News. In the last 10 years, they've taken the White House, the Congress, the courts, and what's left of Zell Miller's mind—and it's only made them madder.

Therefore, tonight, as a solution, I would like to suggest that as a national policy, we encourage the reestablishment of the old Soviet Union. Sure, it was an evil empire, but at least it kept the Republicans *busy*! Who has time for gay marriage or activist judges or brain-dead bulimics when you've got a real bogeyman to freak out about?

The problem with American politics today is that one party has the monopoly on all the anger. To be a Republican is to walk around all day madder than Paula Abdul with a fistful of Vicodin and nothing to wash it down with. And to be a Democrat means—I dunno, your guess is as good as mine.

It seems like ever since Michael Dukakis was asked how he'd feel if his wife got raped and he said "whatever," the Democrats have been the party that speaks softly and carries Massachusetts. When Dick Cheney says "Go fuck yourself," they say "How hard?" In the last election, George Bush called John Kerry a coward, a liar, a wimp, a flip-flopper, and a war criminal, and Kerry got so incensed he almost fell off his Windsurfer. It's bad when the person in your party with the biggest balls is named Teresa.

Democrats would do well to remember this: Anger can be good. Anger can be cleansing. Anger can be a force for change. Anger is what made America what it is today—a hulking pariah whose only friends are toadies and sheiks.

BILL MAHER

NEW RULES

Yawn Jockey

NEW RULE

This year, instead of running a new Kentucky Derby, Kentucky must skip the horse abuse and just show an old one. No one will know the difference. They've been showing the same NASCAR race since 1994, and no one seems to mind.

You, Too?

NEW RULE

Bono is not a banker. Not long ago, Treasury Secretary John Snow suggested U2's Bono was on a possible short list of future presidents of the World Bank. Now, as much as Bono cares about relieving Third World debt, he should always remember that a rock star's place is in the studio or on the stage, not in a bank. Unless it's Axel Rose filling out a loan application for a used car.

Hard Cell

NEW RULE

You can make fun of Lynndie England if you want, but when it comes to prisons, we're all holding the leash. America's anti-sweetheart, Private Lynndie England, has finally faced justice for her part in the Abu Ghraib prison scandal—or as Rush Limbaugh calls it, "the sleepover."

Now, a lot of people think Abu Ghraib happened because, as Americans, we're comfortable asking our horny hillbillies to fight our wars. And we are. But we're also comfortable pretending that anyone in America who winds up in prison for whatever reason somehow deserves not just loss of freedom but a brutalizing, terrifying trip to hell.

It's no mere coincidence that the guard described as the ringleader in the Iraq prison scandal, Charles Graner, worked before the war . . . where? In a prison. In America. He didn't learn to torture from the CIA or Special Ops; he picked up his abuse skills right here and took them to Iraq—outsourcing at its worst!

In a way, we are all Lynndie Englands because we know what's happening in our prisons and we clearly don't care. We tell ourselves the convenient lie that anyone who bears the label "criminal" or "terrorist" is irredeemable, subhuman psycho scum, and so whatever happens to them behind bars is justified, when the truth is that millions of nonviolent Americans have been traumatized for life in our prisons simply because they either did drugs or made a bad judgment, usually when they were young, stupid, and drunk—you'd think President Bush could relate.

There are more than two million Americans locked up, and that is not including the people who work at Wal-Mart. America, the nation that always has to be number one, *is* number one in terms of percentage of its citizens in jail: two million people total. It costs $40 billion to house this many prisoners. Do you know how many countries that had nothing to do with 9/11 we could attack for that kind of money?

In conclusion, if your response to this is "not my problem," remember this: There are monsters and animals in our prisons, yes, but most didn't go in that way, but it is how they'll come out.

Or to put it another way: If you think Martha Stewart had an attitude before . . .

BILL MAHER

NEW RULES